TRANSFORMATIONS

IDEAS FOR THE MIDWESTERN LANDSCAPE

TRANSFORMATIONS

IDEAS FOR THE MIDWESTERN LANDSCAPE

David Van Zelst

with Carolyn Ulrich

Photography by Linda Oyama Bryan

Published by
The Ashley Group
A Cahners® Business Information Company
1350 East Touhy Avenue
Des Plaines, Illinois 60018
847.390.2882   FAX 847.390.2902

Printed in China

Landscape Architects and Designers, Van Zelst, Inc.: David Van Zelst, David Greibe, Greg Rippel, Scott Martin, Derrick Blair, Brian Nacker

Concept & Design: Paul A. Casper
Editor-in-Chief: Dana Felmly
Writer: Carolyn Ulrich
Art Direction: Bill Patton
Group Production Director: Steve Perlstein
Photography: © 2000 Linda Oyama Bryan

ISBN 1-5886204-2-5

First Edition

Acknowledgments

I am deeply grateful to everyone who has helped to make this book a reality.

To my clients, first of all, for their willingness to have their landscapes photographed.

To my dedicated staff and craftsmen, for their consistently fine work in all our endeavors.

Most of all, I wish to thank my wife, Cindy, and family, whose constant support has been so vital to the success of Van Zelst, Inc.

Table of Contents

*S*tone steps create a useful and
beautiful effect among pink and white
phlox in this rock garden.

Introduction

The View from Here
A Midwestern Perspective

Designing landscapes is a great way to make a living. The work is varied, interesting, and rewarding. It doesn't exist in a theoretical world of artistic abstractions; it begins and ends with a client. At Van Zelst, Inc., satisfying the design needs of the client is our first priority.

A HISTORY

When I founded Van Zelst, Inc. as a landscape design/build firm 19 years ago, I knew that it offered me a life I would enjoy. What I could not then envision was how rewarding it would be to work with clients and provide for their landscaping needs. Year after year, we at Van Zelst, Inc. have been designing, installing, and maintaining beautiful landscapes where clients raise their children, entertain friends and build their private histories.

Client satisfaction is based upon the quality of our work and services provided. In whatever we do, my staff and I emphasize quality craftsmanship and quality materials, both in hardscape and plants. Regarding plants, for example, we now grow 90% of the perennials we use because this is the best way to ensure that they are well-developed and healthy. We also grow selected trees and shrubs.

Our headquarters in Wadsworth, Illinois, is not a typical corporate complex. Along with the usual equipment facilities plus the 60 polyhouses where we grow perennials, we have a design studio where our landscape architects and support staff work. Intentionally styled as a gabled American home, the studio building offers clients a means of seeing how a wide variety of plants appear in a home-like setting. The surrounding landscape typifies our varied capabilities.

TEAMWORK

We work as a team. Each design is the result of a collaborative effort among the landscape architects and other specialists. Our methodology is termed "design/build," which means that one landscape architect serves as team leader and supervises the entire design, construction and installation process. When many different subcontractors are working together on a complex installation, it is simpler and less confusing for everyone, including the client, to have one person responsible for all aspects of the work.

Installation of a new landscape often begins with extensive excavation and earth removal. There are occasional surprises. Once we found a car. Another time we uncovered a group of 12,000-year-old mastodon bones and tusks in a marsh at the headquarters site. "If it's buried, we'll find it," is our in-house joke.

"O fie! 'Tis an unweeded garden that grows to seed."

— *William Shakespeare*

A landscape is not finished the minute we complete installation. Landscapes and gardens need time to mature. Often two or three years pass before a project fully achieves the look that the design team intended. Hence, we stress the importance of good maintenance. A landscape that is not expertly maintained will deteriorate and be a disappointment. At Van Zelst, Inc., quality design, quality service installation and quality maintenance are the bedrock of the company philosophy.

THE INDIVIDUAL APPROACH

We also pride ourselves on our individual approach to design. Each project is unique, and that is our intention. I do not want to have a "signature" style, nor do I want a "cookie cutter" look, wherein the same few plants are used and all the designs are similar. Instead, we work diligently to satisfy each client's wishes, whether for a small colorful flower garden, an estate with grand sweeping views, a private retreat or a formal French-style parterre. All of the residential work displayed within this volume was designed and installed by Van Zelst, Inc.

Our design process is equally individualized and geared to the specific interests, dreams and desires of the client. Following our initial conversation, after which we photograph or videotape the site, we make preliminary designs and return for further discussions. We may also visit during different times of the day in order to assess such matters as the changing light or the way certain shadows fall. How we work depends on the project.

Art cannot be measured. Nor can an artist point precisely to the source of an idea. Sometimes solutions for a design problem flash instantly to mind. Sometimes concepts evolve gradually. There is no common thread other than an approach that starts with visiting the site and analyzing its specific needs. The only thing we know is that, for each project large or small, our work begins and ends with the client.

T. David Van Zelst
Landscape Architect

American Beauty

Creating a distinctive landscape in a just-built suburban subdivision is a special challenge, even when the setting is a small, picturesque lake. It may be beautiful, but it's bare. And the owners who moved into their new Glenview house wanted it to have all-perennial borders, privacy screening, a vegetable garden, a formal herb garden, a rock garden, a patio, and a fountain. Since their children were small, they also needed a play area within sight of the house and, most important, a totally secure enclosure.

THE EXISTING SITUATION

The lawn was unusable, consisting of a thin layer of topsoil over nearly impenetrable fill. The lot had also served as a construction storage area while nearby homes were being built, and included a 10-inch thick gravel road that had to be removed and regraded. The slope leading down to the lake rendered the yard less than congenial to children's play.

Lavender globes of Allium giganteum tower over the dark purple spikes of Salvia 'May Night' for a display of thoughtfully orchestrated color in early summer. The white wooden fence provides a light-hearted, typically American framework for seasonal floral displays.

We began our work, therefore, from the ground up, raising the grade of the back yard by taking soil from the slope, leveling the yard, and amending the soil to make it more hospitable to grass and the plants we wished to grow. To provide privacy and to block the view of neighboring houses, eight 15-foot tall spruce were planted along the back. Numerous shrubs were then added to simulate the naturalistic effect of a woodland edge.

Next to the house, however, the feeling is formal. Here, a gracious bluestone patio provides ample room for grilling, entertaining, dining, and children's play. It's the place where the family spends most of their time. Just off the patio, a classically-inspired herb garden provides all the basil, oregano and parsley the owners' culinary hearts could desire. Comprised of four boxwood squares, each with a seasonally-planted stone urn in the center, the herb garden area is paved with a brick path that leads to the garden's focal point: a white-flowering clematis vine clambering up the wall.

The lawn, reconfigured to provide for children's play, extends to a gracious arched seating area at the rear of the property. A focal point of the garden when viewed from the house, the arch provides a spot for relaxation and meditation. A crabapple tree stands near the arch.

In early spring, masses of red tulips accented by yellow daffodils anchor a planting of purple grape hyacinth (Muscari). The bulbs stand in sharp relief to the neatly edged lawn.

THE ROCK GARDEN

In spring, hardy bulbs abound—daffodils, tulips, crocus, muscari and hyacinths among others—providing a welcome jolt of color to the winter-starved soul. Enhancing the bulb display is a judicious use of groundcovers like the evergreen creeping thyme, not yet in bloom, and creeping phlox (Phlox subulata), which is. A rock garden was constructed along the steps leading down to the waterfront, and here the brilliant pink and white phlox make a dramatic show. Later in spring, the purple spheres of Allium giganteum float over the rock garden area (pages 8 and 9).

Steps of chunked limestone provide a rustic, natural look to the rock garden and lead to a deck that was built partly to serve as a dock for fishing and paddle boating. It is the owner's favorite spot. From the deck, the view extends along the shoreline, which has been planted with perennials, shrubs and additional clematis. Swimming serenely on the lake is a pair of white swans. Residents year-round, thanks to an aerator that keeps a portion of the lake ice-free, the swans were introduced partly as a deterrent to geese. The cygnets that hatch each spring are eventually moved on to other lucky lakes.

A formal French-style garden appears primarily ornamental but is really a working herb garden. Located adjacent to the patio, the garden permits the owners, who enjoy outdoor cooking and entertaining, to quickly pop over and snip just what they need for their latest creation.

A *moment of serendipitous beauty occurs as the large white panicles of oak leaf hydrangea (Hydrangea quercifolia) blush with the pink hues of nearby daylilies(Hemerocallis). The long-lasting hydrangea flowers will eventually turn a dusty rose. Daylilies are available by the thousands in a rainbow of colors. Both are excellent plant choices for the Midwest.*

Generous plantings of annuals and perennials thrive on both sides of the white fence where flowering bulbs filled the space during spring. The undulating fence line adds a welcome sense of movement to the design.

P rominent along the lakeshore is the custom-designed white wood fence that lines the perimeter of the property. Wood was chosen for the fencing since it seemed to best match the style of the house with its white-frame windows as well as provide a cheery backdrop for the plantings. There's no better accent for a free-spirited American garden than a white wooden fence.

The Little Details

Although the splendid views of the gardens against the backdrop of the lake are its crowning glory, many special details add to the landscape's charm. Just off the patio, for example, a small granite millstone fountain provides the soothing sound of trickling water and attracts birds, much to the delight of the owners' children. Water for the fountain is pumped from the lake and then returned.

When summer turns to fall, the garden is transformed into a kaleidoscope of oranges, reds and yellows. The large Norway maple tree near the birdhouse and the burning bush at the left contribute much to the vibrancy of the scene.

A large classically-inspired urn serves as a centerpiece in each of the four boxwood-enclosed squares of the herb garden. Plantings change with the seasons. Here red geranium, trailing vinca, helichrysum and spikes highlight the garden in summer.

The plants were also placed with care in the borders. In late spring the purple blooms of the towering Allium giganteum are echoed by the deeper purple of 'May Night' salvia. In summer, as the white panicles of oakleaf hydrangea (Hydrangea quercifolia) begin to blush with hints of pink, the effect is enhanced by the pink-flowering daylilies growing alongside. A gate opens to reveal a rosy rhododendron, standing before the visitor like a welcoming sentinel. Little magic moments like these make a garden special.

Beautiful from the beginning, the landscape is now beginning to achieve a look of lived-in maturity. Just four years after they moved in, the owners have achieved everything they wanted. From bare bones to a landscape that has it all.

"Lucky is the gardener who has learned first-hand and early that Nature is outrageous everywhere..."

— *Henry Mitchell*

The welcoming open gate invites views into the autumn garden. The deep green of the conical arborvitae provides contrast to the variegated hosta and light-colored shrubs.

Written in Stone

Not every day does a French-style house, complete with turret and traditional slate roof, come into a landscape architect's life. It's a rare joy when it does.

AN OLD WORLD CHARM

Good design always aims to integrate landscape with architecture, but a house with distinctive features poses special challenges as well as special delights. In this case, the shape of this Wilmette house, the roof material, and its unique ornamentation offered clues on how to proceed.

The house was well-placed on the property and seemed to sit comfortably in the space. But we wanted to draw attention to its individual beauty and also to enhance the European, Old World ambiance it conveyed. A seemingly minor choice, like selecting gravel as the material for the new driveway rather than asphalt or concrete, is one example of how we gave the entire aspect of the landscape a more European feel. Many of the grand gardens of England and France are lined with broad gravel walkways.

Irregularly shaped flagstone, laid in the brickwork of the house, was repeated in the curving brick sidewalk. Although recently designed and installed, the sidewalk appears to be the same age as the house.

Another European touch is the crabapple tree, espaliered against the front wall. Espalier, the technique of training a tree's branches horizontally or in a fan-shaped pattern, is a means of producing fruit in an extremely limited space on a flat surface. Perfected by the French in the 19th century, it's a fitting detail for the setting.

FRAMING THE HOUSE

A major choice was the decision to use a wide array of specimen plantings to set off and frame the house. Serviceberry (Amelanchier), a native woodland tree with four-season interest, was one of the woody plants that we selected, along with large numbers of other shrubs and ornamental grasses.

All of these plantings are displayed in curving beds that swirl around the perimeter of the property, replicating the curve of the turret. The lawn, too, is shaped as a grand sweeping curve. Such design elements may remain unrecognized by many visitors. However, they play a large part in creating the landscape's overall look of coherence and grace.

Attention to details is crucial to the success of any landscape design; here the architecture offered us the opportunity to do something truly unique. The house, which is built of beige brick, includes an inlay of large irregularly shaped flagstones embedded in the facade. This unusual facet of the ornamentation gave us the inspiration to repeat this motif in the curved walkway that leads up to the front door.

Low, neat plantings of clipped boxwood and vinca wrap around the walls at the front of the house. A specimen planting of the multi-trunked serviceberry (Amelanchier) will change with the seasons and offer a pleasing form in winter.

The striking house, with its turret and uneven stonework in the facade, evokes an antique French chateau.

Purple crocus and red variegated tulips make the early spring garden a feast for the eyes.

Laid with contrasting brick, the sidewalk now includes flagstones shaped exactly like those on the wall. Van Zelst, Inc. always aims to make a newly installed landscape appear mature, but that's not always possible. In this instance, however, it's truly hard to tell the difference between the new and the old.

THE PATIO

Moving from front to back, we approach what we consider the high point of this design-the raised patio, which continues the theme of restrained elegance. Constructed of tumbled Brussels block, the patio exemplifies yet another design choice that relates landscape and architecture. The hardscape material for the flooring and side walls is very similar to the gray of the house's slate roof. A children's playhouse in the back yard is also topped by a slate roof—one more example of the stylistic coherence of house and garden.

Another simple yet effective detail makes striking use of the hardscape used in the patio. Just to the right of the patio and providing a transition to the side of the house is a cluster of the Brussels block pavers that lie recessed in the turf grass so that they create a modified checkerboard configuration. Known informally in the Van Zelst office as an "exploding pattern," it is more correctly called a design of "pavers with turf joints."

In the rear of the house, a Brussels block patio becomes the landscape's dominant feature. Pavers recessed in the lawn link the patio to the side of the house and also allow additional room for socializing when the owners entertain al fresco.

A playhouse in the rear mimics the style of the main house with its rounded French-style door, window box and slate roof.

$\mathbf{A}$s the grass grows around the pavers, the design acquires an aged look, contributing to the sense of permanence we desire.

But the recessed pavers are also functional. Since the back yard is not large, one of our design challenges was to make it feel and appear larger than it really is. The owners needed to have ample space for outdoor entertaining, so when large numbers are expected, the pavers now offer a gathering place and provide room for spillover from the patio.

SPACE-SAVING MEASURES

We further addressed the matter of limited space by planting three columnar maples at the back of the lot. Tall trees but narrow, they provide screening and greenery without taking much room from the garden. The lawn area is restricted, but since the owners have children, it was essential to retain a portion for a play area. The back yard is mostly shady, but there is still enough sun on the patio for sun-loving seasonal annuals and a small kitchen cutting garden of herbs.

By careful attention to the strengths of the site and then designing around weaknesses such as limited space, we were able to create a newly installed landscape with an established, classic look. By playing off the architecture, we were able to incorporate detailing that is not only original but unique.

The view to the street from the front of the house passes over newly planted viburnums, hostas and conifers.

Slopes and Curves

The Van Zelst company headquarters is not your typical corporate complex. Ensconced on a semi-wooded site in northeastern Illinois, it has as its heart a recently constructed design studio building that suggests a traditional American house with a gabled roof. The setting is not coincidental.

A HISTORY

Nineteen years ago, when I founded Van Zelst, Inc., everyone worked in a metal pole barn. As the business expanded, 15 people were jammed into a 1,000 square foot office. Since employees are the key to any business success, I believed it was important to build a space that would be congenial and comfortable for them.

I also wanted to be able to demonstrate to clients what we could offer them. Here, in this quasi-residential setting, we have incorporated many elements of our projects, which focus primarily on private homes. The landscaping of our office directly illustrates our style, our love of color, our preferred plants and the way we plant them in mass groupings. It's a place to browse and get ideas.

In spring daffodils and other hardy bulbs cascade down the slope in front of the Van Zelst, Inc. design studio.

Drivers whizzing by on Highway 41 may see snippets of color or glimpse a rolling lawn surrounded by tightly planted borders. Those who stop for a closer look will see how those elements have been integrated as a total design.

The studio building sits atop a modest slope encircled by perennial borders, with the meticulously maintained lawn flowing gently downhill to the highway. A planting of honey locust and maple form a mini-grove at the base of the hill, offering welcome summer shade to visitors stepping in from the parking lot. It is also a habitat for the hostas, oak leaf hydrangeas and fothergilla sheltering beneath their branches.

UPON ENTERING
THE BUILDING

From the parking lot to the front door, a walkway of red brick pavers swoops up the hill in a wide, gracious curve, offering ample time to appreciate the daffodils, peonies and bright pink spirea that may be blooming alongside. Plants are clustered for increased impact, not dotted about or laid out in a line.

The Van Zelst, Inc. design studio is surrounded by ever-changing mixed borders of shrubs, perennials and annuals with impeccably maintained lawn. Here, spikes of yellow-flowering yarrow and the white bell-like blossoms of our native Illinois Penstemon digitalis billow in the breeze.

At the entrance, broad semi-circular brick steps invite visitors to turn around and survey the countryside to the east. Large curving beds on either side of the front door extend the length of the building and then turn the corner, suggesting a stroll around to the side. The plantings are bold, consisting of grouped conifers, grasses, and giant hostas, accented by interplantings of flowering daylilies, salvia or seasonal annuals. In the back, conifers, deciduous trees, and a tall wooden fence block views of the company's industrial section. This area houses trucks, sheds and the polyhouses, where we grow the majority of our perennials as well as some shrubs and trees.

THE FOUR-SEASON GARDEN

One planting in particular merits attention. The back of the building is U-shaped, so for the small inset we designed a formal garden of boxwood and ornamental grasses with vinca as groundcovers. The combination of formal clipped boxwood hedge and tall dancing grasses makes for an exciting formal/informal mix. It's a truly four-season garden, since the boxwood and vinca are evergreen, while the plumed grasses remain standing until they are cut down in March. The design is easily adaptable to any limited space, but would be particularly attractive in an urban townhouse setting.

The bright pink flowers of the 'Neon Flash' spirea turn this well-known shrub into the showy star performer of this wide border planting.

The headquarters complex was intentionally designed to resemble an American home surrounded by lawn and ever-changing display gardens. Seen here: the gabled design studio building in autumn with the yellowing plumes of fountain grass (Pennisetum) in the foreground and a nearby maple, already a brilliant red.

When viewed from inside the building, this little garden becomes even more interesting, and serves to remind us how important it is to design landscapes that can be seen from inside. In the upper Midwest, five months of the year are spent primarily indoors. We need to plan for that to make sure we don't spend those cold months staring out the windows at bare ground. Here at the office, a pair of tall spruce and a honey locust planted by the back fence provide a focal point, drawing the eye over the boxwoods to the grasses and then to the tall trees. One more proof that a very small garden can have a big impact.

The design studio rises in the distance, seemingly an organic part of the slope on which it was built. Judiciously placed conifers and large deciduous trees punctuate the open space.

Woodlands adjoin the Van Zelst, Inc. headquarters and contribute to the year-round appeal of the site. Tall conifers and ornamental grasses add year-round interest. A tasteful fence screens views of the equipment area.

"The landscaping of our office directly illustrates our style, our love of color, our preferred plants and the way we plant them in mass groupings."

The landscaping at the office, like that in most of our designs, was planned for a progression of eye-catching color and contrasting textures. Even when the growing year is winding down, the changing autumn colors offer exciting contrasts in unexpected places. Hostas, for example, become a multi-colored rainbow of yellow, orange and green and make a beautiful complement to the orange-red leaves of serviceberry (Amelanchier) or maple. Other hostas turn a rich bronze.

DESIGNING FOR MULTI-SEASONS

Autumn is also the time when the ornamental grasses truly come into their own, providing valuable height, structure and movement to a landscape that is losing many components of its design. Then, as well, decorative rocks become more prominent as solid forms against which the dark, round seed heads of coneflowers and rudbeckia stand in graphic contrast. As winter closes in, these structural elements become increasingly important.

Designing for multi-season interest in a variety of landscape situations is the Van Zelst trademark. Designing with a free-flowing yet informal style is another. But whatever the size, whatever the individual style of a client's landscape, our prime concern is always quality-of materials, of workmanship and of design. Our display gardens portray these principles in action.

The handsome pattern of the brick paving catches the eye as one ascends the walkway to the design studio, flanked by 'Neon Flash' spirea. Yellow daylilies can be seen in the background.

Georgian Asymmetry

It suggests an English country estate from the 18th century, but this suburban Chicago property is all-American. Built in the 1920s directly on the shore of Lake Michigan, it includes a red-brick Georgian-style mansion, a lawn grand enough for the display of several sculptures, and a view of the lake that's unsurpassable.

DESIGNING FOR TWO

Since the predominant characteristics of Georgian architecture are symmetry and balance, one very reasonably expects that the landscaping will follow suit. An important aspect of our work here, however, lay in the way subtle asymmetrical touches were incorporated into the design without detracting from the overall sense of stability and order. Another major endeavor revolved around a unique feature of the site: the fact that it appears to contain two houses. Indeed, when originally built, it did. Now the houses are separately owned, but the lawn still flows seamlessly from one front yard to the other, expanding the sense of grandeur and space for both. One of our tasks was to devise ways of distinguishing the two properties while also keeping them visually united.

A gently curving brick walk in front of the house is lavishly planted with an array of summer-flowering perennials such as rudbeckia, purple coneflower and daylilies.

51

The view from the street merely hints at the pleasures to come as the house, screened by a stone wall and balustrade, is glimpsed through the iron front gate. A long curving path, constructed of red unit pavers, leads to the rear of the property where the house sits, flanked by a patio and courtyard, and fronted by planting beds on either side of the entrance. On the east side of the property, bordering the lake, a tall hedge of mixed shrubs provides windbreak and helps to showcase the sunken garden that is a principal design feature. Along the street side, a massive American elm shelters the plants that thrive in its shade—astilbe, coral bells, hostas, pachysandra, ferns and ligularia. As one steps up from the street, the astilbe and coral bells frame views of the house with a soft touch.

The owners asked for "No corners, no straight lines," and their wishes have been respected, both in the hardscape and in the plantings. At the entrance to the house, for example, the pavers used in the sidewalk are configured into a circle that fans out and then continues in a relaxed swoop towards the patio. Two large planting beds are also curved and filled with groupings of loosely swaying Russian sage, purple coneflowers, and daylilies that mingle with the more sedate boxwood and pachysandra. The beds do not match. Plants on one side of the walk may not find a partner on the other. The entire facade of the house with its plantings and hardscape is a demonstration of what might be termed "balanced asymmetry."

The property includes several works of art, including "The Lovers," the sculpture shown here in the sunken garden.

The outdoor rooms also fit this concept. A courtyard on the left and a patio on the right are both circular spaces of roughly the same size but are not identical. The trees, a deliberate mix of old and new, do their own balancing act. Special treasures to be retained include the giant elm by the street along with an old spruce and some crabapples by the front entrance. Additions included the Fox Valley river birch (Betula nigra), Japanese maple and mugo pine, all selected as large plants that would immediately be more in scale with the size of the house.

The flower beds in front of the house form a subtly relaxed contrast to the more severe Georgian architecture of the house.

ART IN
THE GARDEN

The patio provides space for dining and relaxation plus enchanting lake views. Since it faces the east, it seemed the perfect site for the owners to install a shimmering bronze sculpture of three dancing figures entitled "The Dawns." Because of a glass wall on the eastern side of the house, many dawns as well as the sculpture can be viewed year round.

Early morning sunlight casts warm light over the patio, which faces Lake Michigan.

"The Dawns" already existed on the site when we began our work. A second sculpture, created from imported Spanish stone and entitled "The Lovers," stands by today's sunken garden. Both are serious works that raise the issue of how to integrate art into a landscape. It's important in these cases not to choose plants that are unusual or likely to pull attention away from the art. On the other hand, sensitive plant choice and placement can serve to enhance a work's visual impact. If there is no focal point in a particular setting, plants can be used to establish one.

THE SUNKEN GARDEN

The setting of the patio, while lovely, could also be breezy. So we installed a sunken garden along the eastern border of the property as an alternative setting for outdoor relaxation. An old English design feature, the sunken garden probably evolved from an 18th century peculiarity known as the ha-ha, which was little more than a super-long ditch. While the 18th century ha-ha was used to eliminate fences and make one's property appear endless, the purpose of this sunken garden is to provide privacy for the owners. With additional help from a slight berm, the garden can barely be seen from the neighboring house.

The interesting circular pattern of the brickwork at the base of the front steps demonstrates the important role played by hardscape in landscape design. Containers and statuary add further interest to the space.

Intimate seating areas such as this bring a human scale to a property marked by magnificent architecture and a grand front lawn.

As the seasons change, a wide array of perennials come and go in the garden. Lilies, peonies, iris, catmint (Nepeta) and lady's mantle (Alchemilla) arrive in early summer. Daylilies, coneflower and globe thistle (Echinops) appear later. Following the English practice of planting the crevices of their stone walls, creeping phlox (Phlox subulata) and low-growing sedum was inserted amidst the stonework.

Although the mixed hedge that runs along the sunken garden provides nice screening and a windbreak, it restricted views of the lake. We decided therefore to remove a few shrubs at selected points and make openings or "walk throughs" so the owners could step out to the balustrades and their own private overlooks. A subtle touch, the openings are not easily seen in a casual stroll through the space, but they add much to the enjoyment of the property.

Quality landscape design always works hand-in-glove with the architecture of a site, and when that architecture is Georgian, certain parameters are already set. Balance and order are important, and symmetry is assumed. But it is possible to enliven a balanced framework with occasional asymmetrical touches—the planting beds at the house entrance, the curving walkways, the sunken garden—and little surprises like the secret walk-throughs. In so doing, the design serves the architecture but is never its slave.

A shady area offers the opportunity to grow hosta, ligularia (flanking the stone path) and astilbe (in the distance).

Big Color in a Small Space

A garden does not have to be large to be grand.

For proof, look no further than the Knightsbridge Wine Shoppe in Northbrook, Illinois, where the flower garden and surrounding landscaping enchant all who pass by. As an award-winning wine shop, Knightsbridge is a place that the owner insisted must "look outstanding every day of the week." He also requested a host of welcoming flowers, "since gardens make people feel friendlier and happier." At that time, the landscaping at the shop consisted of two yews and a sidewalk.

The shop is housed in a rectangular beige brick building with a simple, restrained facade and windowless side walls. It is located near busy streets and a commercial district but stands alone.

THE CINDERELLA EFFECT

The task was thus to design a dazzling landscape for the pleasure of visitors and to establish a distinguishing first impression. Since a high percentage of the wine shop's business is conducted from October through January, it was important that the design provide four-season interest as well.

The Knightsbridge Wine Shoppe enjoys a non-stop display of vibrant color from early spring to late fall. Blues and purples predominate in early summer as dame's rocket (Hesperis matronalis) and Salvia 'May Night' set the scene.

The Van Zelst plan called for a 40 by 20 foot semicircular flower garden directly in front of the building as a way of softening the entrance. There would be vines and roses on the side walls, a high quality lawn and clipped yew hedges to provide some screening of the parking lots. The simplicity of the lawn and hedges would allow the bold multi-colored hues of the flower garden to stand out, like actors on a stage, and be the true stars of the performance. The space between the shop and the flower garden featured a preexisting piazza patterned from squares of red brick and gray stone. The oversized terra cotta containers we placed on both sides of the door echo the hues of the pavement in homage to the Mediterranean and wine country.

FROM THE GROUND UP

A high quality lawn and flower garden, however, require high quality soil, the opposite of what we found on site. It was therefore necessary to start by completely removing the existing very poor soil and replace it with a new mix of leaf compost, mushroom compost and topsoil. Only then could planting of bulbs and perennials get under way.

The flower bed in front of the Knightsbridge Wine Shoppe was configured as a softly curving semi-circle to soften the straight geometry of the architecture.

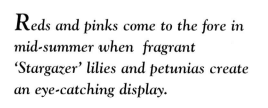

Reds and pinks come to the fore in mid-summer when fragrant 'Stargazer' lilies and petunias create an eye-catching display.

When those bulbs, a multi-colored melange of crocus, daffodils, tulips and hyacinths shoot up in spring, their bright sunny yellows jolt the spirit and send it soaring. For vibrancy, we stressed flowers in shades of red, purple and pink.

A COLOR SHOW

As the season changes, so do the colors. A visit in early summer will find the garden brimming with blues and purples as clusters of dame's rocket (Hesperis matronalis), spikes of Salvia 'May Night', pansies, and petunias establish a tone of serene elegance (blue being considered the aristocrat of garden colors). Contrast comes from the pinkish bells of Penstemon 'Husker Red' with its maroon foliage, the vibrant hues of coral bells, and an underlying evergreen carpet of sedums.

Visit one month later and the show will be entirely different. Now the pinks of phlox and purple coneflower, the yellows of rudbeckia and daylilies take over. Autumn will usher in the bronze and russet tones of chrysanthemum accented by selected asters. Non-stop color everywhere.

Oversized terra cotta planters filled with seasonal plantings and jasmine trees line the entrance to the wine shop and help to impart a Mediterranean ambiance.

Pink petunias and the yellow-green flowers of dill make an unusual but effective match. An edible herb, the dill also attracts monarch butterflies to the garden.

In autumn, brightly colored pink chrysanthemums contrast dramatically with the yellowing leaves of a honey locust tree (right), and grape leaves (below).

The oversized containers lining the building facade also contribute to the drama, offering bulbs, seasonal annuals and mums in turn. Serving as focal points in this symmetrical display are the two giant pots of non-winter-hardy jasmine flanking the main door. These treasures are "boarded" in a greenhouse during the winter and return in spring.

BUILDING A RAINBOW

Along each side wall, sturdy 4 by 4-inch posts reach to the top of the building and secure wires that have been stretched up and across at wide intervals. From this matrix emerges a planting of clematis and roses on one side and—most appropriately—grape vines on the other. These have by now matured sufficiently to etch interesting dark patterns against the bare white surface. A few feet away, a meticulously pruned crabapple curls upward, adding its own brush strokes to the wall's elegant calligraphy.

Although Knightsbridge is a commercial setting, the garden that was installed here could be translated for any small residential site. Principles and philosophy do not change with the job. Quality—whether of design, installation or maintenance—is always important. However, individual elements acquire added significance when space is limited.

Designing for a small space poses special challenges, but it also offers special rewards.

Small can be more than beautiful. It can be spectacular.

Woodland
Grandeur

The great European landscape designers of the 17th and 18th century were not concerned with flowers. They thought instead of land, water and trees. They thought in terms of broad sweeping lines, which they brought into being by moving a river here or shaping a hill there. The point? To create the perfect view, framing a subject that would ennoble the soul or edify the mind.

PROTECTING THE LAND

The New World we live in affords few opportunities for such grand undertakings. Most landscaping efforts have more modest aims. But the owners of a 15-acre estate in Barrington, Illinois, had a long-term interest in protecting the integrity of their land. This led Van Zelst, Inc., to create a modern American take on the landscaping hurly burly of centuries past.

The approach to the house, perched on a gentle slope, leads up a long curving driveway that allows the eye ample time to sweep across the vast rolling lawn to the right and to appreciate the screen of pines, spruce, serviceberry and witch hazel bordering the wooden fence to the left. A 20-foot-wide horse trail that runs along the fence is maintained as a mulch bed, a testimony to the owners' serious interest in preserving the long-term health of these trees.

Formal gardens near the house give way to a vast woodland area planted with thousands of perennials and a meadow-like panorama of color. Tall trees provide striking vertical accents to the landscape's fundamental horizontality and permit sufficient light for the perennials to thrive.

The house itself is fronted by an assortment of woody material and seasonal flowers with a patio, swimming pool, tennis court and formal garden in back. A subtly curved pergola leads to the swimming pool, and an arched opening indicates the way to the informal grounds beyond. While the carefully sculpted formal garden is classically French in character, the expanse of swooping terrain recalls the great landscape gardens devised by the English.

From the house, the land rolls slowly downhill to a lowland area and a quiet stream that is part of the region's flood plain. Ancient cottonwoods and other stately trees tower over the water and make for beautiful reflections, best seen from a bridge, which was designed to appear as a settled presence in the landscape. Beyond the stream, the land moves sharply upward.

FINDING A VIEW

The opportunities for ennobling views abound. Whether standing on the curved bluestone patio looking down or from the bottom of a slope looking up, one never ceases to find a focal point—sometimes the house, sometimes an expertly sited tree, at other times the water with its reflections.

An arched opening offers a transition from the formal hedged garden near the house to the woodland meadows beyond.

In mid-summer, daylilies carpet the sunnier parts of the woodland area. Their orange hues contrast dramatically with the pinks of the coneflowers.

73

The views didn't just happen. The flood plain area was originally choked with eight acres of buckthorn, which was painstakingly hacked away. In order to open up the sight lines, 25 trees up to 40 feet tall-spruce, white pine, ash, crabapple-were moved and replanted at the perimeter of the property. In the wooded areas on the slopes, meadows were established with thousands of spring-flowering bulbs and perennials such as purple coneflower, daylilies, coreopsis, liatris, astilbe, dianthus and salvia. In all, 38,000 bulbs plus 50,000 perennials and woody plants were added to the property.

The gracious brick residence sits atop a low hill with views in many directions. Large old trees, expertly pruned, frame the view towards the house.

Foot paths also play a part in guiding the eye. In the meadow area, a curving mulch path leads uphill through the trees and opens into a view of the adjacent pasture with a herd of horses as the occasional focal point. And as older trees in the meadow areas succumb to age, they will be replaced with 12-inch caliper trees in order to maintain the sight lines and the appearance of maturity.

The woodland's ancient trees, awe-inspiring at any time, become magical when touched by the early morning sun.

75

A mixed border in summer includes ornamental grass, annuals and perennials. Masses of yellow daylilies and 'Goldsturm' rudbeckia set the cheerful tone, accented by swaths of red.

This look, which we term "organized informality," stands in stark contrast to the obviously designed formal garden, pool, and patio areas adjacent to the house. Here, an interplay of precisely placed circles and curves relate the various elements of the space into a coherent whole.

THE USE OF BLUESTONE

The gracious curved patio, laid with bluestone and adorned with elegant urns, sets the design theme, and leads to the formal French-style garden where yew hedges are meticulously clipped into four round-edged enclosures. Inside each space a variety of garden plants are grown. Since the area is gradually becoming shadier as trees mature, the plantings are not identical in the four

In spring, yellow-green leaves, newly opened, stand in handsome contrast to the darker greens of conifers in the background and the pine on the left.

beds. Hosta, ligularia and astilbe thrive in the shadier spots while daylilies and rudbeckia occupy the sunnier ones. Although these plants are all perennials, they may be moved as the situation dictates. Annuals such as begonias, geraniums and impatiens fill in for season-long color.

Bluestone is used throughout for the patio floor and extends from the patio into the formal gardens and on to the curved-end pool, which was designed to replicate the lines of the patio and the yew hedges. The outside walls of the patio and the garden, plus the pillars of the curving pergola that leads to the pool, are all of red brick.

Wood is used for accents such as the archway that caps the opening leading to the meadows and lawn.

The entrance to the swimming pool is marked by an arched brick pergola topped with wisteria.

Plantings across the estate have been orchestrated with views of the house in mind.

Ｒight below the archway, another deft touch: a bluestone circle that is followed by flagstone steps and casually arranged stones. Here, in the transition area between formal and informal, a planting of low sedums and creeping thyme fill in the space between the stones, giving the arrangement the look of a miniature rock garden. Strawberries add a touch of whimsy to the mix.

Grandeur is not usually the American way with landscape. But in a setting such as this, it has been possible to combine the elegance and serene views of ages past with the informality and relaxed feel that the American lifestyle requires. Cultivating this garden has indeed turned into the best of all possible worlds.

Winter beauty lies in the details. Here, branches of winterberrry, our native deciduous holly (Ilex verticillata), lie sheathed in snow that makes its brilliant red berries even more striking.

Low plantings and high trees soften the view of the brick residence. The cheerful yellow blossoms of Rudbeckia 'Goldsturm,' seen here in the foreground, bloom over an extended period during the summer.

Serenity on a Busy Street

Treading in the footsteps of the famous is a daunting task. How do you respect the past and yet reshape it to meet current interests and needs? And if the person whose work you are charged to "improve" has actually been a formative influence, the stakes increase enormously.

IN THE STEPS OF A MASTER

Several years ago, the grounds of this contemporary Winnetka home were designed by the German-born landscape architect Franz Lipp, also the designer of Cantigny Park in Chicago's western suburbs. There was an ample lawn in back, modulated by berms and outlined by a collection of conifers that had been planted to provide privacy. The effect was austere but serene.

Originally a ranch style structure, the house had seen many changes until it reached its present incarnation as a gracious low-slung contemporary, at least in front. In contrast, the rear of the house had become a dazzling configuration of angled glass panels soaring to the sky.

A circular perennial garden, outlined by a low boxwood hedge, offers informal plantings within a formal structure. In mid-summer, the bright red flowers of bee balm (Monarda) capture all attention.

The owners realized they needed to restore the landscape since some of the conifers had weakened or died. However, they insisted that any changes respect the integrity of the original design. Ensuring their continued privacy was also a prime concern. Fortunately, the assignment came in at a time when our next available landscape architect was someone who had once worked in Franz Lipp's Chicago firm.

STARTING WITH THE TREES

During the initial phase of the project, we brought in a wide selection of new conifers, including hemlock, white pine, arborvitae and white fir. We also introduced white birch, a tree the owners had grown to love in travels to Michigan's Upper Peninsula. To add colorful accents and textural interest, we selected a number of deciduous flowering shrubs and small trees. Using the forest green conifers as a backdrop enabled the white trunks of the birch and the flowers of the shrubs to stand out more prominently.

A selection of trees and shrubs embrace the facade of the house with contrasting textures and shapes rather than flowers. In autumn, the varying greens change to mesmerizing shades of orange and yellow.

Instead of designing the lawn as a open sharp-edged rectangle, we opted for a gracefully curving outline, created by allowing the border plantings to meander in and out of the space. Pruning—or the lack of it—is another way we softened the overall look of the landscape. The owners dislike the heavily rounded "gumball look" in gardens, so woody plants have been allowed to naturalize and follow their own inclinations.

Two slightly curved stone benches provide a spot to relax and enjoy the garden, here with liatris, phlox and coneflower in full bloom.

At the front of the house, the owners preferred restraint and asked for entryway plantings that emphasized varying textures and shapes of green instead of flowers. We planted major shade trees such as honey locust and linden in this area, while smaller specimens like redbud, crabapple, serviceberry and star magnolia serve to form the understory. At ground level there are plantings of broadleaf evergreens—boxwood, Oregon grape (Mahonia), holly—and a lush carpet of pachysandra provides groundcover.

While some trees and shrubs frame the house, others surround a large, centrally located driveway circle which we designed to replace the original plain asphalt parking area. The new driveway circle was constructed of pea gravel embedded in asphalt and edged with bricks. Just beyond the parking area, another circle was developed, this time as a formal-informal flower garden with a fountain as its centerpiece.

The circle garden, connected by a curving brick walkway to the parking area, is enclosed by a low, 18-inch boxwood hedge. Just inside, two semi-circular gray stone benches sit facing a small central fountain. The balance of the garden space is given over to a variety of colorful flowers—pink dianthus, blue salvia, roses, liatris. While the overall structure of the circle garden is structured, the plantings are just the opposite. Shapes and colors are mixed with abandon, and an old rose may be found growing next to a coneflower.

A *small fountain and elegant lotus provide the centerpiece of the circular perennial garden.*

The architecture of the house, restrained in front, becomes dramatically contemporary in the rear.

The fountain is an important element. The sounds of trickling, flowing water soothe the spirits in any garden, but since this property is located on a busy street, the fountain plays a functional role in helping to minimize the noise of traffic. The tall trees and shrubs that run the entire width of the property also help to reduce traffic sounds while ensuring privacy.

The broad, overriding concept of this project was to intermingle the past and present, to blend the old and the new. For the landscape architect, the goal is always to make the line between the two eras appear seamless.

The circles of the fountain garden are echoed in this curved walkway that leads from the parking area to the garden.

89

A Flair for Flowers

This is a flower lover's garden. Unabashedly romantic, it harbors a profusion of flowers, charming antique ornaments and a wealth of sheltering trees. It also projects a decided European flair, since the owners, residents of Holland for several years, had acquired a taste for the ambiance that only a centuries-old culture can provide.

SURROUNDED BY BEAUTY

The rosy-brick house, situated on a gentle rise, faces the street with an arched entry way, a front door decorated with a floral motif, and lace curtains at the shuttered windows. It is surrounded by flower gardens in front and back, although black iron gates on both sides of the house separate the two. Stylistically, the space is united.

Bountiful flower beds swoop through the front yard space, beginning with a pair of oak leaf hydrangea shrubs (Hydrangea quercifolia) that flank the base of the brick paver driveway. With its large oval white blooms, interesting exfoliating bark, and autumn color, the oak leaf hydrangea is a particularly useful plant for northern Illinois landscapes.

Purple liatris and yellow Rudbeckia soften the corners of the patio dining area.

The flower beds continue along both sides of the driveway and fill in the areas in front of the house. Sturdy, quick-growing perennials such as coneflowers, daylilies, ornamental grasses, 'Autumn Joy' sedum and lamb's ears are key performers here, although the beds also include quantities of annual begonias and impatiens. Directly in front of the house, a massive planting of tightly-packed white begonias commands attention while along the driveway, pink is a predominant color. When the pink-flowering coneflowers bloom in consort with roses like 'The Fairy' and white shasta daisies, there is, indeed, something fairy-like about the soft pastel color scheme.

The owners' love of flowers is pervasive and even extends to this floral motif on the front door.

A PASSIONATE AFFAIR

Plants and flowers are a life-long passion for the owners, one of whom is the business manager of a floral design firm, so right after moving day seven years ago, work began to develop a new landscape "with as much flower and plant material as quickly as possible." Everything except the existing swimming pool was torn out, and even the pool needed some work as its pipes lay under the old patio, which was removed.

The homeowners also wanted to experience the illusion that the indoors and outdoors are one, to feel that they are outside even when they're not. Thus, the home's lovely lace curtains hang only in upstairs rooms while downstairs windows are left uncovered. They particularly love to look out from the kitchen or family room, places where they "can feel the outdoors in the house all the time."

The gracious brick residence is surrounded by generously planted flower borders. Here, the greens of ornamental grass and the still-unopened flowers of 'Autumn Joy' sedum provide a soft textural background for the brightly colored rudbeckia and coneflower.

Black iron gates on each side of the house open to reveal the expansive patio, swimming pool and garden area beyond.

Free-spirited coneflowers and refined white begonias set a welcoming tone at the front of the house.

What they see in the backyard includes a spacious patio, a tiled swimming pool, a mixed border of perennials and shrubs, places to relax or eat, and a host of handsomely planted containers. The major elements are configured in curves, even the swimming pool, whose irregularity contributed to a more interesting division of the space than a traditional rectangle would have. In some landscapes the pool needs to be screened. Here, it is a central feature that suggests some serene woodland lagoon. As it happens, the backyard is heavily wooded with a mix of newly planted conifers like white pine and deciduous ginkgo, ash and oak. The owners are pleased that they can't exactly tell where their property ends.

94

The elegant bluestone patio is graced by an assortment of neatly maintained containers, many of them filled with white begonias. Bluestone adds a genteel, slightly antique look and contributes to the European ambiance desired by the owners.

Since the owners enjoy playing the host, the patio is a particularly important part of the garden. Constructed of bluestone, it weaves its way along the back of the house and offers ample room for a number of seating and dining areas. The stone had the mellow appearance of age, even when it was new, and the mosses that grew over time added to the desired country feeling. Black iron tables and chairs contribute their own aura of gentle antiquity as they have been allowed to slowly rust. Victorian wire chairs are a charming accent.

The pool takes up much of the space where a traditional lawn would be situated, but a grassy area runs along the mixed border where quantities of long-blooming 'Annabel' hydrangea do much to establish the "lush, non-formal, romantic, drippy feeling" the owners desired for their garden. They sometimes long for the blue hydrangeas so prevalent in Europe's more maritime climate but realize that with our alkaline clay soils and sometimes frigid winters the white-flowering 'Annabel' is a more reliable choice.

The patio wraps around the rear of the house and encircles the swimming pool, providing ample space for dining and entertaining. White 'Annabel' hydrangeas bloom in profusion, adding to the garden's romantic look.

While the 'Annabels' are in bloom, white is a dominant color, especially in the tidy container plantings of impatiens, begonia and bacopa that dot the patio. But brightly-colored pinks, reds and oranges are present in the tuberous begonias, liatris, astilbe and geraniums that grow here as well. It depends on where you look. The views change significantly with each turn of the head, due in large part to the curving lines of the overall design. With such fluidity, nothing is ever static.

IT'S ALL IN THE DETAILS

Charming vignettes abound. The black iron gate opens to reveal the garden bathed in summer light. A pair of antique chairs meld into a background of multiple greens. A container with an attractive bronze patina displays orange tuberous begonias. A green-on-green arrangement with pachysandra, boxwood, ivy and yews provides the framework for highlighting the multiple trunks of a serviceberry. Seen after a rain or on an overcast day, the various shades of green shimmer in the light and are sufficient in themselves to make a beautiful garden.

The space is a pleasing mix of intimacy and grandeur. Not huge, but spacious, and always charming. It's a garden where the owners, as they say, can "look outside and feel fabulous."

Containers of red geraniums stand out vividly against the bluestone paving. White hydrangeas bloom in the background.

A View
with a Room

A garden exists to make people happy—the people who live with it most of all, but also the neighbors, visitors, and passers-by whose impressions may be brief. Yet, fleeting beauty can have an impact. Even a momentary glimpse inspires, and many fine poems have been the result.

MIXING BEAUTY INTO THE EQUATION

It is ironic, then, to realize that successful garden-making is often more about engineering than poetry, more about technical expertise than romance. Before those exquisite roses can flourish, the soil in which they grow may need to be amended with a truckload of compost. To prevent erosion, powerful machines will carve a hill into strange new shapes. To open up a view, giant trees will be dug up and moved. And a garden next to water will depend on an understanding of hydraulics.

When we developed this particular small garden on a suburban lake, the plan called for an extended, multiple-level deck facing the water. Comprised of three parts, the deck includes a large wooden-floored area with space for dining, a lower level laid with limestone, and another elevated wooden structure, where shade is provided by the mature copper beech tree that rises from an opening in the floor.

A stroll along the side of the house leads to a sudden view of the lake, highlighted by the floral arrangement in an elegant pedestal planter.

As part of the Des Plaines River waterway, the lake experiences fluctuating water levels, so it was first necessary to build a stone retaining wall in the lake to support the deck. We then planted a row of conifers directly in front of the wall to help screen it from the house. Viewing the lake from the deck, one is blissfully unaware of all the deck's structural underpinnings. Nor can they be seen from the street.

PRIVACY PROTECTION

At the front of the lot, the house is all but invisible, screened by magnificent old spruce and pine. With just sufficient turf for the dogs to frolic, this area is primarily an open courtyard comprised of varying shades of green. It gives no hint of the pleasures to come.

The pathway leading down to the lake is richly planted with quantities of annuals and perennials on either side.

Two wooden decks, linked by a stone passage, come alive with colorful in-ground plantings and numerous containers.

Along the driveway, we designed a neat curving border, defined by a low gray stone retaining wall. On the opposite side of the road, a generous planting of mixed impatiens and a gazing ball centerpiece offer a welcoming blast of color.

The walkway that winds towards the house and lake leads into an old-fashioned strolling garden that greets every step with something new. Every square inch seems covered. Judiciously placed trees and shrubs frame the emerging view and direct all eyes toward the lake.

A beech tree emerges through an opening in the wooden floor of the deck and provides welcome shade. Container plantings of annuals contrast effectively with the white-painted surfaces of the deck and walls.

The views from the deck are even more delightful. As one emerges from the sometimes shady approach and steps up to the spacious wooden structure, suddenly, everything beyond is open space and light. Everything dazzles in the sun. Other houses share the lake but remain secluded behind their own shrubberies, feeding the fantasy that one is the master of everything in sight, even the pair of white swans sailing serenely in the distance. It is an enchanting place.

Large conifers and occasional shade characterize the area in front of the house. Here, an undulating stone retaining wall defines the space and sets off plantings of hosta, daylilies, cleome and Verbena bonariensis.

The decks are shaded by the copper beech tree and striped awnings. For extra color, large terra cotta containers brimming with impatiens, petunias, and caladium are tucked into corners here and there. On the lower level stone deck, a narrow border of low, brightly colored annuals grows right next to the house. Since this area receives full sun, the zinnias, marigolds and snapdragons planted here all thrive.

From the house a flagstone walkway leads down towards the lake and a sandy beach. Stroll along the waves, then turn around and see the house in its entirety for the first time. Reflected in the clear blue water of a sunny summer day, it is a lovely sight, pretty enough for a poem.

And there, right down by the water's edge, is the retaining wall, an embodiment of the of technical know-how that makes the whole garden happen. It, too, is a lovely sight.

In the clear light of summer, the house is a serene presence on the lake where a pair of swans also reside. A retaining wall, built by Van Zelst, Inc., shores up and supports the decks and protects them from fluctuating water levels. A planting of arborvitae helps to screen the wall from the house.

Framing
the View

The eye sweeps across the landscape, taking in the cattail marsh, the pond and the woodlands beyond. No fences can be seen, and the vast expanse appears as one continuous estate.

A BORROWED VIEW

The property, comprised of 10 acres, includes a marsh, but it does not include the pond and woodlands beyond it. We applied what is known in landscaping parlance as "a borrowed view."

Using a borrowed view is a time-honored tradition. A designer may cut a space in a hedge to direct the eye towards a distant mountain or move some trees to frame a lovely steeple—perhaps to make a property appear larger than it really is, perhaps merely to take advantage of some exterior loveliness. In this case, the borrowed view served multiple purposes.

The property was originally five acres. When the owners had the opportunity to purchase an adjoining five acres, they took it. They then asked Van Zelst, Inc., to develop a master plan that would integrate the two properties and make them appear as one. We were also charged with developing extensive gardens behind the house and to situate the layout for the swimming pool, gazebo and tennis court, plus the extensive walkways that would connect them all.

By regrouping trees and thoughtfully placing large plants like the Miscanthus shown here, the view toward a distant cattail marsh and woodland were carefully framed.

Flower borders along the broad sweeping walkway present a brilliant summer show of purple Verbena bonariensis and rudbeckia, interplanted with ornamental grasses, such as Pennisetum and Miscanthus.

The approach to the gracious brick house leads from a circular driveway to a parking area with a central, oval-shaped planting island of river birch, pines, yellow daylilies, pink spirea, and wintercreeper euonymous. Just opposite, conifers such as blue spruce, juniper and yew mingle with a variety of perennials to screen and soften the facade of the house with an array of interesting textures. Large numbers of astilbe form interesting patterns against the dark green yew hedge by the front door. Two blue spruce nicely complement the rosy brick of the house, and a nearby sunken garden features a mix of additional woody and herbaceous material. Some of these plantings were pre-existing. Others are being added as the development of this property continues.

THE LAYOUT OF THE LAND

While the front of the house seems enclosed and private, the back gives a feeling of great openness, an expansive horizontal space comprised only of land and sky. This is partly because the garden in the back is entirely new. Many of the just-planted trees, shrubs, grasses, perennials and annuals are still small. Even so, some materials fill in quickly—feather reed grass (Calamagrostis), for example, Verbena bonariensis and Rudbeckia fulgida 'Goldsturm'. And the maples, honey locust and river birch (Betula nigra), which will take years to attain full stature, are already contributing dazzling shades of orange, red and yellow to the fall landscape. Before any planting could begin, one of our first tasks was to regroup existing trees. Conifers such as blue spruce and fir, some up to 20 feet tall, had been scattered about the grounds. By moving them to new locations, some views were opened and the sight lines directed in others, most particularly toward the marsh. Tree placement is always a prime consideration in any landscape design.

The judicious selection of trees with brilliant autumn color, like the sugar maple seen here, will contribute greatly to the multi-season interest of this landscape as it matures. The maple's brilliance is enhanced by contrast with the line of dark green spruce in the background.

The flower gardens flanking the walkway will one day rival the great herbaceous borders of England. The variety of perennials is awesome—dianthus, lavender, coral bells, yucca, yarrow, coreopsis, penstemon, salvia, hardy geranium, catmint, sedum. Annuals such as snapdragons, petunia, alyssum, nicotiana, begonia and ageratum fill in the spaces, while the perennials mature. Small shrubs such as mugo pine and boxwood are grouped in clusters of five or six, and add structure along the way.

Curved and circular beds near the swimming pool are also filled with flowers and ornamental grasses. Here, mass plantings of Verbena bonariensis, fountain grass, purple coneflower (Echinacea purpurea), and catmint (Nepeta) are already filling in their allotted space and creating dramatic effects. In addition, the verbena and coneflower attract monarch butterflies, while bees gravitate to the catmint. This garden is both beautiful and environmentally friendly.

This view towards the marsh and woodlands will only increase in beauty with the passage of time.

As always, thoughtful details make a space more interesting. Large, rounded containers filled with seasonal flowers and grasses create colorful accents beside the house. An unusual bench, formed from a tree trunk, fits in naturally with its surroundings. It also invites views toward the gazebo or the tennis court. In a heavily mulched area, a lighter color of mulch is used for a winding pathway so that foot traffic can be directed away from the flower beds.

Although this project is relatively new, we endeavored to make it appear established. It already has a wonderful country garden aspect, and this will only become more delightful in the years to come.

The massive perennial plantings, just one year old, are linked by equally massive brick paver walkways. The swimming pool and nearby gazebo can be seen in the distance.

Gardens For All

In 1997 and 1999 Van Zelst, Inc. was responsible for the planting of two major projects at the Chicago Botanic Garden in Glencoe, Illinois: the Buehler Enabling Garden and the Circle Garden. In each project, there were strict time and technical constraints as we coordinated our work with that of the other groups. Everything needed to be grown expertly and look perfect.

The Buehler Enabling Garden is a teaching garden as much as a show garden. Beautiful and useful, it displays the latest strategies for helping persons with any kind of disability to continue enjoying and cultivating their gardens. Today, there are over 35,000 perennials, ornamental grasses and other plantings in and around it. Acquiring and installing those plantings were the major challenges of the project.

The Circle Garden was created as a showcase for colorful annuals. However, it's the hardscape design and permanent plantings that provide the stage on which the more temporary players can shine. In the Circle Garden, large numbers of shrubs plus deciduous and evergreen trees were integral to the overall design.

We are proud to be a part of the venture, which so many can enjoy for years to come.

The Circle Garden was designed to showcase an ever-changing panoply of annual plants within a permanent framework of perennials, trees and shrubs. A large pulsating fountain in the center of the space is the garden's dominant feature. Low boxwood hedges surrounded by flowering annuals flank the fountain.

Circle Garden

The Circle Garden, designed by Geoff Rausch of Marshall, Tyler & Rausch, Pittsburgh, Pennsylvania, is located directly west of the Chicago Botanic Garden's Education Center. It is a highly formal space, with a balanced, symmetrical design. Yet the garden is not static. Irregularity and variety are trademarks of the trees and shrubs planted around the perimeter, while the annuals planted within the garden soften the hardscape's sharp-edged lines.

It is logical, when first visiting the garden, to move straight down the main walkway to the center and the large fountain that is its dominant feature. From this vantage point, however, one might well ask "Where's the circle?" The fountain design is based on straight-edged geometry that is precisely echoed by the surrounding brick paving. On either side of the fountain, two secret gardens, both squared rooms enclosed by tall yew hedges, continue the geometric look of the space. It is only by moving outside, to the perimeter of the garden, that its circular framework can be fully comprehended.

The challenge for us at Van Zelst, Inc. was to install all of the permanent plantings within a six-week time frame during the middle of summer. Because summer is not an ideal time to transplant

Alternating squares of 'Chicagoland Green' and Korean boxwood have been clipped to form a low tabletop hedge that draws attention to the rounded forms of the bright pink chrysanthemums seen here. Annuals are rotated throughout the growing year.

The Circle Garden is an enchanting mix of permanent and temporary plants. Tall spruce and false cypress (Chamaecyparis) join weeping hemlocks in providing a stable dark green background for whatever seasonal flowers may appear. Clumps of variegated Japanese iris (Iris ensata) standing at the corners of the boxwood hedges add interest to the planting even when they are out of bloom.

The large central garden, as well as the two adjoining secret gardens, are lined with tall 'Hicks' yew hedges that needed to be installed with exact precision. Seen in the foreground: variegated Japanese iris and the recently introduced Zinnia angustifolia 'Star White.'

woody material, we had to invoke several strategies to ensure the plants would both survive and thrive. We watered regularly and used anti-dessicants to help reduce moisture loss. We also practiced "stage digging" with some trees, such as the crabapples. This means the trees were pre-dug and watered well in the nursery before they were wrapped with burlap and transported. Another source of concern was the site itself, which had once been a swamp. Although drainage problems had generally been corrected, we paid special attention to the height at which we planted. We also amended the soil.

It was essential that the Circle Garden appear established the moment it opened. The 'Hicks' yews that formed the principal hedge were brought in as six-foot tall plants and then sheared to give an instantly mature effect. Some spacing was closer than usual to make the garden appear more filled in. It was also important that the planting be done precisely. With a formal layout such as this, plants had to be placed literally within inches of the exact goal if we were to maintain the symmetry of the design. All of this we accomplished.

"An annual garden is a joyous garden. The flowers are sprightly, and the colors are bright. It is a place that elicits happiness. For us at Van Zelst, Inc. to play a part in the creation of this special space was a source of pleasure as well."

In the secret gardens, sprays of fountain grass (Pennisetum) flank the benches and soften the hard-edged geometry of the square space.

Buehler Enabling Garden

The Buehler Enabling Garden was designed by Geoff Rausch of Marshall, Tyler & Rausch, Pittsburgh, Pennsylvania. It has three separate spaces–a Gallery Garden in the enter, a Container Court to the north, and a Vista Garden to the south. The walkway leading to the principal entrance in the Gallery Garden passes through an informal grouping of tall, multi-stemmed 'Whitespire' birch, which were 20 to 25 feet tall when we planted them. Such large trees were selected because the Enabling Garden needed to look mature on opening day. Spacing plants such as annuals close together also helped to achieve a look of instant maturity.

The long, narrow Gallery Garden, dominated by two central pools and fountains, features parallel raised beds of ornamental grasses and shrubs along its walls. Towering grasses and compact shrubs form a pleasing alternating pattern of colors, shapes and textures. The sounds of flowing water and grasses rustling in the breeze add extra interest.

The Buehler Enabling Garden exhibits a variety of strategies that permit persons with any kind of disability to continue gardening. Scents, sounds and raised beds of varying heights are the hallmarks of this special space.

Sensory pleasures abound when one steps into this section of the garden. Seasonal annuals vibrate with contrasting colors. Giant rustling grasses and flowing water fill the space with sound. Soft, highly textured leaves appeal to the sense of touch. Scents from Nicotiana sylvestris and other fragrant plants waft through the air. Shown at far right: one of the Garden's numerous brick raised beds.

Throughout the garden, and particularly in the Container Court, the walls have been opened for large "windows" with trellises for panes. Perennial and annual vines abound. At ground level, the walls are ringed with two-foot tall raised brick beds that could be used by gardeners in wheelchairs. In each corner of this basically square room, a giant serviceberry (Amelanchier x grandiflora 'Cumulus') stands watch. Because the walls were already built when we came to plant the trees, they were lifted into place by crane.

The Vista Garden lives up to its name. Capped by a pergola and lined with balustrades at its terminus, it offers a view towards one of the Botanic Garden's many placid lakes. Within the space, more serviceberries fill the corners, while stunning wall fountains, vertical wall planters, and three- to four-foot tall raised beds and containers on pulleys bring gardening within easy reach for all. Hanging baskets on pulleys enable an individual in a wheelchair to engage in container gardening.

Because the Botanic Garden is a living museum, it needs to showcase both common and exotic plants. Finding those plants isn't always easy. We literally went around the world in our search for some of the varieties we wanted. The quest for a particular tree peony, for example, led our project coordinator to northern China. Other plants were procured throughout the United States, with some contract-grown by specialized nurseries, while we grew thousands in our own greenhouses in Wadsworth. Survival of the less-common varieties sometimes dictated that they be grown in custom-blended soil. The Enabling Garden is a complex mix of thousands of plants. But even when flowers are only a memory, it continues to portray the beauty and off-season serenity of the well-designed garden that it is.

The view from the center entry encompasses two low pools and low raised beds planted with alternating ornamental grasses and shrubs. Trellis walls and windows endow the space with a sense of openness but also provide a place for growing vines.

Purple coneflower (Echinacea purpurea)